ECK Wisdom

on

Relationships

ECK Wisdom

on

Relationships

HAROLD KLEMP

ECKANKAR
Minneapolis
www.Eckankar.org

ECK Wisdom on Relationships

Printed in USA

Photo of Sri Harold Klemp (page 74) by Art Galbraith
Cover painting by Susan Sarback
Third printing—2020

Library of Congress Cataloging-in-Publication Data

Names: Klemp, Harold, author.
Title: ECK wisdom on relationships / Harold Klemp.
Description: Minneapolis : ECKANKAR, 2020. | "Third printing--2020." | Summary: "Author Harold Klemp, spiritual leader of Eckankar, helps you discover the source of love, the secret of all relationships, how to love yourself, and much more" -- Provided by publisher.
Identifiers: LCCN 2020029560 | ISBN 9781570434938 (paperback)
Subjects: LCSH: Eckankar (Organization)--Doctrines. | Interpersonal relations--Religious aspects--Eckankar.
Classification: LCC BP605.E3 K55386 2020 | DDC 299/.93--dc23
LC record available at https://lccn.loc.gov/2020029560

♾ This paper meets the requirements of ANSI/NISO Z39.48-1992 (Permanence of Paper).

CONTENTS

THE SOURCE OF LOVE

*E*verything revolves around love. It always does. No matter how much we rush about in this world and how harried, ambitious, or sorrowful we become, the world stays together for some reason. The reason is God's love.

God's love is the fabric that draws us all and keeps us here. It makes the whole work, even though sometimes it looks like nothing is working at all.

The two supreme laws are: God is love, and Soul exists because God loves It. Very simple.

But how do you make this work out in everyday life?

Whenever you're in doubt about any action, ask yourself: Is it true? Is it necessary? Is it kind? You can also ask, What would love do now?

THE SECRET OF ALL RELATIONSHIPS

*E*veryone has some experience with love—even a child who has a pet kitten or a dog. Soul is trying to give back or respond to God's love that's coming through. In some way the child learns lessons about caring for the pet. If he neglects the pet and it runs away, the child learns one of the first hard lessons about love: If you love something, you have to nurture it.

Like anything else, you have to put your full attention on it. Sometimes in the courting stage, a couple focuses all their attention on each other, but after they are married they begin to take each other for granted. Instead

3

of looking at each other when they talk, their eyes drift. Maybe the man is thinking about work, and she is thinking about things happening in her life. They talk past each other.

During courtship when two people are looking at each other very directly, there's the power of love in the gaze of one human being upon his beloved. They can actually feel the power in it.

But later when the partners become distracted and put their attention a foot above each other's head, the nourishing power of love, or the ECK, doesn't come through to nurture each other. This is often when their relationship begins to die a slow death that can take many years.

If you love someone or something, nurture it. That means, at least once during the day, give the object of your attention or the person of your heart your full love. Even if just for a little while, listen to what they are saying. During this time, you are putting the little self aside.

The little self comes forward to meet the problems of the day, but put it aside to take time to just listen, love someone, and put your full attention on them, face-to-face. It's directly looking at the person you love, even after you are married. This is when the nurturing occurs and when the relationship is strengthened.

THE CONNECTING POWER OF LOVE

One morning a couple were having breakfast together before the wife left for work. The husband, whom I'll call Ed, had the day off and planned to spend it at home. His wife, Maggie, ate quickly and rushed out the door, saying that she had to stop at the post office on her way to work.

As soon as she drove off, Ed noticed that Maggie had left her reading glasses on the table. He knew she would be upset when she discovered she had forgotten them, because she wouldn't be able to do her work. But since he had no car that day, he didn't know how he could help.

Ed and Maggie are both members of Eckankar. Ed had often heard other ECKists talk about the inner communication that exists between people who love each other and love God. This seemed like a good time to give it a try. He sat down, closed his eyes, and attempted to send a mental message to Maggie: "You left your reading glasses at home. Please come back and get them."

But a mental command doesn't have the power of the spiritual voice, which is picked up instantly through the direct perception of Soul. Mind is slower than Soul; mind often runs into blocks when trying to transmit or receive messages, even between loved ones. Ed could sense that his message was not getting through to his wife.

He closed his eyes once more, but this time he did not try to send any messages. Instead, he went into contemplation and thought of nothing except the love that he had for Maggie. He concluded by saying to Divine Spirit, "Give my love to my wife."

A few minutes later Ed heard a car pull into the driveway. He looked out the window and saw that it was Maggie. This was unexpected—he thought she would be well on her way to work by now. As she came in the door, he said, "Did you know that you forgot your reading glasses?"

"No," she said, giving him a surprised look. "I just decided to bring you some newspapers to read, so you'd have something to do during the day."

The underlying element here was divine, unconditional love. There was also a deep love for someone who was precious and dear. Ed was trying to reach Maggie because he loved her, and she responded to the love by going out of her way to bring him the newspapers. Love was the factor that enabled them to connect with each other through the invisible lines of communication.

The ECK (Holy Spirit) works this way in the daily lives of many ECKists. There is inner communication between the ECKists, and the connecting link is always love. Because there is a bond of love, the ECK can work.

Strengthening a Marriage

*O*ne day I went to a grocery store, and an ECKist I'll call Jim was working there unpacking vegetables and fruits. As he worked, we talked. He asked, "What are some ways to strengthen a marriage?"

So while I looked through the potatoes, I tried to think of a good answer for ways to strengthen a marriage. I said, "Learn to forgive and forget the small slights that take place in every relationship."

And I said, "Don't press each other's buttons." An argument usually starts in a family because the two people know each other so well, and they know exactly how to get their mate upset. So when there's an argument, they talk about exactly those things. They figure that's what an argument is for.

The third thing I mentioned was, "Practice silence on days when your mate is having a bad-hair day." I had finished my answer, so Jim went his way in the store, and I went my way.

Then I turned the corner, and I heard this big, booming voice. It was Jim's supervisor. He was a very stocky man, built like a rock. He was wearing a T-shirt that said "Center of the Electromagnetic Universe." He looked as if he could have been the center—very strong.

He was writing on a clipboard. Apparently, he was working with Jim, seeing which fruits and vegetables were in low supply and needed to be reordered. Then he made a mistake. He took his pencil and started erasing furiously on his pad. Then he said, "The best, most useful invention of mankind—the eraser!"

And I thought that was a down-to-earth answer to Jim's question: The best, most useful invention of mankind—the eraser! If you make a mistake, erase it. If someone else makes a mistake, erase it from your memory. This was Golden-tongued Wisdom speaking to Jim very directly.

God's love in action—look for it everywhere because it is all around you, all the time. It is God's love flowing to you. And when Soul becomes aware, It finds that It must always return this love to the divine source from which it came.

You are Soul. Learn your purpose in life, which is to become a vehicle for this divine love.

PAST LIVES AFFECT OUR RELATIONSHIPS TODAY

$\mathcal{T}$he play of karma underlies all human relationships.

In this next story, a young man we'll call Nick gets to balance the scales of justice from the past. He needed to repay a victim from a previous life, but the Mahanta, his inner guide, sent a dream to prepare him for the necessary, though painful, experience.

Nick had a dream in which a beautiful young woman came to the office. She was trying to use the phone on his manager's desk. Nick and the girl felt an immediate attraction for each other in the dream, and soon they began a passionate romance. But, to his frustration, it led nowhere.

Then he awoke.

Some weeks later, a young student came to the office to get work experience. Nick loved her from the start. He did everything in his power to win her heart, but she coyly brushed aside his passion with promises. Later, always later. Soon everyone in the office was talking about their relationship.

Then the sky fell in.

Through the office grapevine, Nick learned that this young woman had been having a secret love affair with his best friend at work. It had begun nearly the first week she had arrived there. Worse, Nick had set the stage. One night that first week he had to work late, so he asked his good friend to take her home. That was the beginning of the end.

Only the ECK, Divine Spirit, kept Nick from losing his mind when he learned of the secret love affair. But he turned sour on life. Why had this beautiful young woman come—to purposely bring him grief?

In his anxiety and anger, he even forgot about the spiritual love of the Mahanta, the Living ECK Master.

Then came a second dream. The Mahanta took him on the Time Track and showed him a past life in which he had been a woman. Married to a wealthy man, this individual had two house servants, both of whom suffered due to Nick's misuse of position and authority. One was this student.

"You made that karma," the Mahanta explained. "That debt stands between you and God's love. Pay now and be done with it."

In the end, Nick recognized the hand of karma and the long-outstanding debt that he needed to settle. It took a while for the crushing pain to subside, of course, but now he's happy he settled the debt. After the pain had finally gone, Nick felt a new sense of freedom and lightness. God's love could now shine more directly into his heart. That obstructing block of karmic debt was gone.

The Truth about Soul Mates

*T*he time-twin, or Soul-mate, theory has no grounding in the spiritual teachings. The masculine and feminine principles are within each one of us. But such a division, or separation, is a phenomenon of the lower worlds and does not exist in the higher ones.

Let's look at the origin of the Soul-mate theory.

The Soul-mate theory arose because some people in early history were quite aware of an emptiness inside themselves. An individual with strong masculine forces driving him might feel an insensitivity to things. So he searched for a Soul mate with whom he'd feel like a whole being.

All that changes during Self-Realization. When an individual reaches the Soul Plane, the masculine and feminine principles unite within him. Then he is made whole.

Once you know the truth about this Soul-mate theory, you can save yourself a lot of heartache in selecting a mate.

A Technique to Help Break a Pattern of Poor Relationships

*L*et's see if we can shed light on personal relationships gone bad.

On a single sheet of paper put the names of all the important people with whom you've had relationships in your life. List two categories under each: *attractions* and *final weak points*. In other words, what about each person attracted you to him or her? Be both honest and fair.

Then look at each to see what it was about them in particular that caused a parting. There is a gap between what you think you're getting and what you finally end up with. You want to close the gap between illusion and reality *before* you invest too much heartache in the relationship.

I've known people with the uncanny ability to choose three alcoholic mates in a row. Maybe it wasn't so surprising since they looked for their companions in drinking establishments. Not one of these people realized they were always fishing in the same water, using the same bait. No wonder they kept coming up with the same kind of fish.

To turn around a life that's so often upside down, the individual must first make an honest inventory of all the factors that have caused the trouble. It's too easy to blame something outside of us for our troubles, especially if we do not like what we see in ourselves. But fixing the blame elsewhere will not make the trouble go away.

Please be objective in your analysis of the people in your life. Otherwise you're no better off than when you started. Are you a loving, giving individual? Then you must learn to find someone who is worthy of that love.

When you finish the list of people, take another sheet and write "Arguments" at the top of it. Again, list the same people. Try to put down the thing you and each person mostly argued about. Was it outside relationships? Were any of the arguments about money? List all of the subjects of disagreement with each person. That list should tell you something about yourself.

The answers you come up with on your list can help you see the next step in changing the conditions of your thought so that old patterns of the past can be broken and give you a fresh promise of a better future.

WHAT GOES AROUND COMES AROUND

By mistake, one afternoon a boy we'll call Toby left his new watch at the swim club. It had been a very expensive gift from his parents. So the family piled into the car and drove back to the club in the hope that they'd find the watch. But, of course, it was gone.

Toby's mother wanted to show him how very angry she was with him for losing the watch. As they came into the house, she stopped to slam the door. But somehow her own watch got tangled in the door as she slammed it. She got a bad bruise.

The pain was so intense that all of a

sudden a realization hit her: This was instant karma, and she was being very unfair to her son. She apologized to him and told him how much she loved him.

When we begin a negative train of thought, Divine Spirit steps in quickly. If you continue in your anger, the lesson escalates. But if you're paying attention, the chance to make it right comes just as quickly.

If you can make it right, you have advanced on the spiritual path.

LIFE'S BEST TEACHERS

*P*eggy (not her real name) is an ECKist who worked with a man who seemed to take great pleasure in insulting her. Some people in this world form friendships by making fun of their friends. It's a strange thing.

One day Peggy went to a restaurant with her coworkers. The man began to insult Peggy in a friendly way. She decided she couldn't take any more. Normally she's a quiet, soft-spoken person who hardly ever shows anger. But this time she flared up.

"If you couldn't insult me," she said to the man, "you wouldn't be able to think of one thing to say." The man was shocked.

She got really angry and kept at him, talking louder and louder until people in the restaurant began looking around to see who was causing such a scene.

After the man and his wife had left, Peggy stood with her husband and a friend out in the parking lot. "You were right to defend yourself," the friend said. "If he can dish it out, he'd better be able to take it."

"You're a saint to have been able to put up with him all these years," added her husband.

As they were talking, Peggy's eyes kept going to a particular license plate on a nearby car. The license plate was enclosed in a frame, and on the bottom of the frame were the words "love their faults."

The friend continued, "Maybe this will teach him a lesson." And the license-plate frame caught her eye again: love their faults.

Finally it hit her. Peggy started laughing. Her husband and the friend couldn't understand why she had suddenly gotten over her anger.

"Look at that license-plate frame," she pointed. "The ECK is trying to tell us something."

The whole license-plate frame read "Geologists love their faults." But she had read just the bottom part of the frame, "love their faults."

Peggy knew it had been right to draw the line with this coworker, but she felt she could've done it with love instead of anger. Because when we act with anger, we're acting from power. And when we act with love, we allow the other person to understand how we feel.

We let the other person know that he is not necessarily bad, but we do not want him to practice that sort of behavior in the future. Otherwise he will lose our friendship. It's very clean and very unemotional. It takes the anger out. It's spoken with love, the kind of love that is called charity in the Christian Bible.

Life's best teachers are the people who toss thorns in our path. So long as it makes us sore, there's a spiritual lesson that pleads for an airing.

The people around you are in your company for give-and-take. Let's say you shrink from the presence of a certain individual. Look at it from the other side. For good or ill, your mutual dealings are bringing changes to both parties, even if ever so slight.

Look behind the screen. What is really going on?

Furthermore, once the karma between you is satisfied, your association will wither on the vine, like a cucumber without water. Karma is just that exacting.

Karma's deck of cards deals both hearts and clubs, friends as well as enemies.

Your dear ones are old friends. You've

been together before. You've tasted the good times and bad, the victories and defeats, the joys and heartaches. Together you gained in spiritual ways. At other times, though, you managed to trip over each other's feet, crying aloud in pain. Then you drew apart. But your hearts did mend. Your friendship was the stronger for it.

Enemies and friends act like spiritual coaches. They round out the rough spots in Soul's unfoldment.

The Mahanta teaches through others. So pay careful attention when sparks fly, because some important thing in you—perhaps courage or forgiveness—needs some polish.

A Spiritual Exercise for Keeping Your Balance

If people do things that upset us, it means that we're losing our balance. And that means we're going to do some foolish thing that's going to cost us in the end. So why do it? Why let the emotions take us over, cause us to do some stupid thing and create more karma? And it will usually be bad karma. So why do that?

HU is an ancient name for God. It is sung as a love song to God and can be sung by anyone of any faith. When you chant *HU*, often the Inner Master will come to you and give you a perspective. Often the Master will say, "Hey, this stuff has been going on for centuries. And it's going to go on for centuries more."

Lord Acton, the British historian, said, "Power tends to corrupt and absolute power corrupts absolutely." If you recognize that this is part of the human condition and can accept it, if you can learn to adjust your life so that you're not always underneath the crushing wheels of power struggles, if you can do that and keep your wits when all around you others are losing theirs, then maybe you've gained spiritually in this lifetime.

These things are the realities of everyday life. These are the things that test Soul. These are the things that test you.

Sing *HU* to yourself, or sing it out loud if no one's around. HU can protect. HU can give love. HU can heal. It can give peace of mind. That doesn't mean forever. It just means that if you face a crisis of some kind or another, remember to chant *HU*.

YOUR BOND OF LOVE WITH ALL LIFE

*I*f you have a pet, you are aware of the bond of love between yourself and your pet. This bond of love exists because you are Soul—a particle of God sent here to gain spiritual experience. Ultimately, to learn how to give and to receive divine love.

What most people don't realize is their pet is also Soul. Animals are Soul too.

Soul exists because God loves It. It's very simple. And when two Souls set up a bond of love, it is stronger and more enduring than eternity. It doesn't matter if the two Souls are human beings or if one of them happens to be a bird, a dog, a cat, or another animal form.

31

You, me, our pets—we are all Soul dwelling here in the world of nature. Nature itself reflects the laws of ECK, the Holy Spirit. We can observe the working of Divine Spirit in the habits of birds, the cycles of plants, and the instincts of reptiles and mammals.

All sing the glory of God; all teach the secrets of life.

In this next story, you'll see how.

Celene (not her real name) is from Trinidad. She felt as if her life had gone to hell in a handbasket. Her marriage had just broken up. Then her son began using drugs.

Life was pretty hard, so much so that one day, while she was driving to work, tears began pouring down her cheeks. She decided to pull the car off the road and just cry.

She pulled up beside a field where young horses were grazing. Still crying, Celene got out of the car to enjoy their beauty.

Suddenly one of the horses stopped what he was doing and came galloping toward her.

He came right up to the fence where she was standing. Then he raised his head and looked directly into her eyes.

An incredible stream of love flowed from the horse to her.

Once Celene understood the gift of love had been passed to her, the horse shook his head, snorted, and trotted back to the rest of the herd.

Animals had often been a means Divine Spirit used to bring love to this woman. She recognized this was the blessing of the Holy Spirit bringing comfort to her. It was a gift from the Mahanta.

Celene further realized there is no need to *speak* love with people, animals, or plants, but just *be* love. If you are love, then the person or animal you love will know.

WHEN A LOVED ONE DIES

A woman I'll call Donna found Eckankar after her son Justin's death in a motorcycle accident. She was very close to her son. Devastated by her loss, Donna was unable to find comfort at church. She regularly cried through the entire service. If only there was a way to feel closer to God, then maybe He would help her understand why the accident had occurred. More important, where was Justin now? Was he all right? She constantly prayed for help.

Five months later, while at her lowest ebb, she had an experience that changed her life. At first, she thought it was merely a dream, but it was actually Soul Travel.

Donna awoke in vivid consciousness in the other worlds. A bespectacled woman with grey streaks in her dark hair met her, and they talked for a few minutes. "Do you know my son Justin?" she finally asked the woman.

"Of course I know him," said the woman. "He lives right over there in that white house." The scene was a normal setting of cottages, such as near a lake resort.

Donna and Justin had a long conversation. He assured her his health was better than it had been on earth. Then looking closely at her, he said, "I know what you're doing to yourself. Please stop. You're only hurting yourself." Before they parted, she asked to hold him in her arms, since she didn't get a chance to do so before his death. Laughing, he said, "OK, Mom."

Soul Travel had put her right there with her loved one. She could actually feel him in her arms. Then she awoke.

Justin's scent still lingered with her, and a peaceful, happy feeling lasted for weeks before it began to fade. Donna was now determined to learn where he was. Somewhere on earth, she knew, somebody had the answer. That's when her sister introduced her to Eckankar. The first book she read was *The Spiritual Notebook*, by Paul Twitchell, the modern-day founder of Eckankar. It convinced her that here was the answer to her prayers. Here was an explanation that made sense.

Grief for her son still overtakes her on occasion. She wants the Mahanta, the Living ECK Master to help her regain the peace felt while with her son during Soul Travel. So she does the Spiritual Exercises of ECK daily. And she directs her efforts to seeing the Light and hearing the Sound—keys to the secret worlds of God.

A Spiritual Exercise to Open Your Heart to God's Transforming Love

*L*ove is hard because we make it so. The uncertainty about being loved shapes the way we act toward others. Some of us are rebellious to the things that our families hold dear. Others of us go to another extreme. We love and nurture others to the neglect of our own well-being. Time often gets us back on track, though.

So what can you do to get back on track as soon as possible and be happy?

One cannot buy love through caring for and nurturing others. Those two qualities can be of the real kind if they come from someone who is a magnet for love.

Look at others as if they are carriers of God's love to you. In fact, they are. The next point is important. You must consciously open your heart to God's love, which is always and forever flowing out to you like a quiet mountain stream.

It's easy to do.

Let's make a spiritual exercise for yourself. Sing *HU*, and, in your mind and heart, watch this quiet stream of God's love flow gently into your heart and being. It will change you.

Your Relationship with God

One day an ECKist I'll call May was telling a Christian friend an insight her friend had probably never thought of. And I would say many Christian theologians have never thought of it either. But it's an extremely good point.

May said, "Soul is like a painting that God painted. Each painting is beautifully unique, and God is invested equally in all of us. Soul is an expression of God. In each case, God did Its best in creating us, because it's not in God's nature to turn out a shabby piece of art."

And May went on. "God loves us as much as Jesus. The reason Jesus stands out so prominently and shines so brightly is that he loved God back equally."

I think that's a very profound insight on the difference between Jesus and many people. But I must say here that true Masters all have this love for God that is equal in returning the love that God gives them. They give this love back to everything around them—to mankind and all living things.

Remember, if you're reading this book, you probably came into this lifetime with a particular goal. And that goal was to learn the secret of life.

The secret? God is love. But you probably knew that already. So what's keeping you from truth? It's the realization, not the knowledge. Knowledge is just a mental thing. But it's the realization that you are Soul. That you are worth something. Because God loved you first.

Once this becomes a realization in you, you will find yourself helping others. Not because you feel you are of the nobility help-ing the trash down there, even though you veil it in nice words: the *poor*, the *children*, using all those nice words which are based on emotional values. But when you have the realization, the true realization, of what *God is love* means, then you're just willing to serve others because you love them. You love them because God first loved you.

You exist because of God's love. So does your neighbor. And if your neighbor needs help and you can give it, you are also help-ing yourself.

We know that we are here to go through purification as spiritual beings. This is the spiritual purification that's necessary so we can one day become a Co-worker with God.

Being a Co-worker with God means to work in the different levels of heaven or even here on earth, bringing divine love to people who are in need. Sometimes it's as simple as just listening to a person who's in trouble or giving something to someone in need. Or if there is a catastrophe in some part of the country, sending blankets and money.

This is being a Co-worker with God. You do this without expecting anyone to pat you on the back and say, "Well done, thou good and faithful servant."

Life doesn't often provide people to come along to pat you on the back and say something like that. But you can be the person who pats someone else on the back and says, "Hey, nice job. Glad you're here. Thanks for your help." And remember to say "I love you" to your loved ones.

We're so busy just with the survival of our human self that we sometimes forget to be grateful for the very dear things in our lives—our loved ones, our mates and our children, our parents, and our brothers and sisters.

SOUL'S YEARNING FOR LOVE

$\mathcal{S}$oul yearns to return home to God. Home to God means the area of supreme divine love that has no conditions attached to it: unconditional love.

So often when we speak of love in a human sense, we don't see the difference. Sometimes our parents say they love us, and then if we don't do things exactly their way, they'll give us the cold shoulder. Or our mate might do this, or we might do this to our mate.

Giving someone the cold shoulder is not unconditional love. It's conditional. And it's a form of control.

It's not true love at all. It's saying, "I

want to do it this way, and you're not doing it my way. So until you do it my way, I'm not going to love you. I'm not going to talk to you."

Eventually the little argument blows over, and everybody is happy again and forgets until the next time.

The next time the relationship between these two people comes to a test and there is no meeting of minds and hearts, this same thing occurs. There will be some way that the two estrange each other. One of the two will give the other the cold shoulder or in some other way harm the relationship—whatever a person can do to say, "You're not doing it my way. Therefore I'm going to withhold my love from you."

It's conditional love. It's human love, not divine love. And human love is people's attempt to be godlike, whether or not they're conscious of it.

I think it is very important in this life to learn to love someone more than yourself—whether it's another person or a pet.

And before you can love someone else more than yourself, you begin by first loving yourself. Even Christ said, "Love thy neighbor as thyself." Right away some people think this means love your neighbor and forget all about yourself.

Loving yourself doesn't mean to have a high, egotistical regard for yourself or go strutting around like some dictator. It means to have respect for yourself as Soul, as a child of God—or as we say in ECK, as a light of God. Because once you recognize yourself as Soul, as one of these beings of God, you've made an important step in your spiritual unfoldment.

The next important step is to know and recognize that other people are also Soul, lights of God.

Love is the goal, then, of our spiritual search. The way to God is ever within the heart, within the loving heart.

QUESTIONS AND ANSWERS

As spiritual leader of Eckankar, I get thousands of letters from seekers of truth around the world. All want direct and useful answers about how to travel the road to God. I reply personally to many of these letters.

Here are several questions I've been asked about love and relationships.

Read on for clues that may help you.

A Technique to Help You Communicate Better

Can you help me with any advice on how to keep the love flowing in my marriage? It's been strained lately.

47

Communication is a difficult thing to keep open in any marriage. One useful technique when things get strained is for one person to interview the other for twenty minutes, with notes.

The interviewer is free to ask whatever he wants. The only limitation is no question can be phrased so that it can be answered with a simple yes or no. That doesn't open communication.

The interviewer is not able to defend himself against any accusations but must sit there and take it. Of course, the roles change in twenty minutes. The other spouse then becomes the interviewer of hopes and dashed dreams.

It is surprising what marriage partners learn about their companions that make them truly interesting people with goals too.

How to See If a Relationship Is Worth Developing

How does one know if a relationship is based on love and is worth developing?

No one has the final word on love, but consider the following points in deciding if you really love someone:

1. Does he bring joy to your heart when you think of him?

2. Do you want to make him happy?

3. Will you love him for what he is and not try to change him? Will you let him be as he is and not what you want him to be?

4. Young people tend to fall in love with their ideal of love. This means that one has the ideal of a Prince Charming who is really a toad. Not all Prince Charmings are toads, and not all toads are Prince Charmings.

5. Don't forget your self-worth. How does he treat you—like a treasure or someone to be used?

Love is the expression of the ECK, Divine Spirit, on earth, and these points should give you a fairly good opportunity to see what kind of relationship you are in.

Is Sex Spiritual?

What is the purpose of sex from a spiritual perspective?

The deep relationship between a couple is a sacred token of human love. The sex urge does not lift anyone into the Soul Plane, so why endorse sex as a means for spiritual unfoldment?

This relationship between mates must be open and clean, without guilt or shame. If you cannot love your family, how will you then love God? The dirt and guilt that the orthodox religions put upon lovemaking is for control of the followers. Guilt and fear have been deeply impressed upon them for centuries.

Lovemaking, a deep expression of love and warmth between mates, is their private business. Overindulgence in anything is lust. Will we be pulled down to the common level of the animal? The union shared by a couple demands mutual responsibility.

Dreams as Advisers

I have been having recurring dreams which involve me, my boyfriend, and another woman. In all the dreams, my boyfriend treats me like extra baggage and ignores me while paying attention to her.

We have been having difficulties in our relationship, and for some reason, I don't trust him. How can I tell whether my dreams are intuitive or simply represent my insecurities?

A relationship without trust won't last. What is the source of this mistrust? Does he look at other women when you are out together in public?

Dreams can prepare you for a relationship that may be coming to an end. They will tell you something is wrong. If your partner is showing less affection toward you, you must decide whether to try to patch up the relationship or let it go.

Think of your dreams as advisers. They may point out problems and offer solutions, but consider all the facts before deciding on any important issue. Especially watch people's daily behavior toward you. Your dreams may suggest what behavior to look out for, but don't break up a relationship without some physical evidence to back up your suspicions.

No matter what happens with this relationship, try to be a greater channel for divine love. Love will overcome suspicion, which can destroy any relationship.

When Children Ask about Divorce

How can people find out whether they love truly or not, and why are they hasty to get married? Why do I find myself in my family instead of another family, and what can a child do to keep from suffering so much when their parents divorce?

Love is blind and probably always will be. The only way to find out anything in life is to go ahead and get the experience. Nothing is ever lost. Each experience can teach us valuable lessons about ourselves, painful though they may be.

Impatience and blindness (a lack of experience in such matters) are the reason for hasty marriages. There's little that can be done about it.

Why are you in your family and not another? It's for the simple reason that you and your family agreed to it before this lifetime ever began. Somehow, all of you saw a spiritual reason for being together. So in contemplation ask the Mahanta to show you what some of those reasons were. It will make you a person of more love, wisdom, and compassion.

How to keep from suffering so much when parents divorce? Love the parent you're with, with all your heart. In other words, fill yourself with love for all who are with you now, this minute, this hour.

What Is True Marriage?

What does the marriage bond signify spiritually?

The marriage bond can only be sacred if it is sacred to the two individuals who have agreed to this union. If they are one in heart, how can they be divided? At their marriage, one couple in Eckankar made a "first cause" statement to each other. They made a vow to help each other in conscious spiritual evolution, out of love, to reach the heights of God.

A true marriage has commitment by each person. Both realize the responsibility of that commitment. A marriage of the heart lets each of the couple remain an individual, but the two are as one.

A Spiritual Exercise to Draw You Closer to God

$\mathcal{T}$ry this simple spiritual exercise to help deepen your relationship with God.

Go somewhere quiet. Sit or lie down in a comfortable place. Put your attention on your Spiritual Eye, a point just above and behind your eyebrows. With eyes lightly shut, begin to sing a holy word or phrase, such as *HU*, *God*, *Holy Spirit*, or *Show me thy ways, O Lord*. But fill your heart with love before you approach the altar of God, because only the pure may come.

Be patient. Do this exercise for several weeks, for a limit of twenty minutes each time. Sit, sing, and wait. God speaks to you only when you are able to listen.

NEXT STEPS IN
SPIRITUAL EXPLORATION

- **Try a spiritual exercise.**
  Review the spiritual exercises in this book or on our website. Experiment with them.

- **Browse our website: www.Eckankar.org.**
  Watch videos; get free books, answers to FAQs, and more info.

- **Attend a spiritual event in your area.**
  Visit "Eckankar around the World" on our website.

- **Begin your journey** with the Eckankar spiritual self-discovery courses that come with membership.

- **Read additional books** about the ECK teachings.

- **Call us:** Call 1-800-LOVE GOD (1-800-568-3463, toll-free, automated) or (952) 380-2200 (direct).

- **Write to:** ECKANKAR, Dept. BK67, PO Box 2000, Chanhassen, MN 55317-2000 USA.

For Further Reading
By Harold Klemp

The Spiritual Exercises of ECK

This book is a staircase with 131 steps leading to the doorway to spiritual freedom, self-mastery, wisdom, and love. A comprehensive volume of spiritual exercises for every need.

ECK Wisdom on Conquering Fear

Would having more courage and confidence help you make the most of this lifetime?

Going far beyond typical self-help advice, this book invites you to explore divine love as the antidote to anxiety and the doorway to inner freedom.

You will discover ways to identify the karmic roots

of fear and align with your highest ideals.

Use this book to soar beyond your limitations and reap the benefits of self-mastery.

Live life to its fullest potential!

ECK Wisdom on Dreams

This dream study will help you be more *awake* than you've ever been!

ECK Wisdom on Dreams reveals the most ancient of dream teachings for a richer and more productive life today.

In this dynamic book, author Harold Klemp shows you how to remember your dreams, apply dream wisdom to everyday situations, recognize prophetic dreams, and more.

You will be introduced to the art of dream interpretation and offered techniques to discover the treasures of your inner worlds.

ECK Wisdom on Health and Healing

This book is rich with spiritual keys to better health on every level.

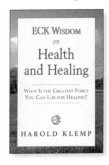

Discover the spiritual roots of illness and how gratitude can open your heart to God's love and healing.

Simple spiritual exercises go deep to help you get personal divine guidance and insights.

Revitalize your connection with the true healing power of God's love.

ECK Wisdom on Inner Guidance

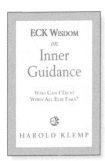

Looking for answers, guidance, protection?

Help can come as a nudge, a dream, a vision, or a quiet voice within you. This book offers new ways to connect with the ever-present guidance of ECK, the Holy Spirit. Start today!

Discover how to listen to the Voice of God; attune to your true self; work with an inner guide; benefit from dreams, waking dreams, and Golden-tongued Wisdom; and ignite your creativity to solve problems.

Each story, technique, and spiritual exercise is a doorway to greater confidence and love for life.

Open your heart, and let God's voice speak to you!

ECK Wisdom on Karma and Reincarnation

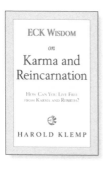

Have you lived before? What is the real meaning of life?

Discover your divine destiny—to move beyond the limits of karma and reincarnation and gain spiritual freedom.

This book reveals the purpose of living and the keys to spiritual growth.

You'll find answers to age-old questions about fate, destiny, and free will. These gems of wisdom can enhance your relationships, health, and happiness—and offer the chance to resolve all your karma in this lifetime!

ECK Wisdom on Life after Death

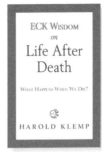

All that lies ahead is already within your heart.

ECK Wisdom on Life after Death invites you to explore the eternal nature of *you*!

Author Harold Klemp offers you new perspectives on seeing heaven before you die, meeting with departed loved ones, near-death experiences, getting help from spiritual guides, animals in heaven, and dealing with grief.

Try the techniques and spiritual exercise included in this book to find answers and explore the secrets of life after death—for yourself.

ECK Wisdom on Solving Problems

Problems? Problems! Why do we have so many? What causes them? Can we avoid them?

Author Harold Klemp, the spiritual leader of Eckankar, can help you answer these questions and more. His sense of humor and practical approach offer spiritual keys to unlock the secrets to effective problem solving. Learn creative, time-tested techniques to

- Find the root cause of a problem
- Change your viewpoint and overcome difficulties
- Conquer your fears
- Work beyond symptoms to solutions
- Kindle your creativity
- Master your karma, past and present
- Receive spiritual guidance that can transform the way you see yourself and your life

ECK Wisdom on Soul Travel

Where do you go when you close your eyes?

Nowhere? Are you sure?

What about when you daydream?

You go places, don't you?

What about when you close your eyes at night—and dream? When dreams seem more real than everyday life?

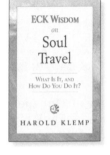

That's Soul Travel. It's a natural process that opens the door to the incredible universes where we truly live and have our being. You are Soul, a divine spark of God. The more attention you give to this wonderful truth, the closer you get to the very heart of God.

You learn how to grow in love and awareness. And that's what life is all about, isn't it?

ECK Wisdom on Soul Travel gives you tools to experiment with and introduces you to a spiritual guide who can show you the road to your infinite future—a road that courses through every moment of your daily life.

Take a peek, and explore your own adventure of a lifetime!

ECK Wisdom on Spiritual Freedom

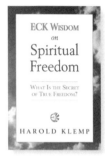

Are you everything you want to be? You came into this life to spread your wings and live in freedom—heart, mind, and Soul!

Author Harold Klemp puts the tools of spiritual freedom firmly in your grasp:

- Keys to embrace the highest expression of who you really are
- Techniques to tap into the divine Life Force for unlimited creativity and problem solving
- New paradigms to reveal the power of loving yourself, God, and all of life

What would you give for the secret of true freedom? Consider this book a ticket to an unexpected destination—the heart of your being.

Open your wings and prepare for flight!

The Call of Soul

Discover how to find spiritual freedom in this lifetime and the infinite world of God's love for you. Includes a CD with dream and Soul Travel techniques.

Past Lives, Dreams, and Soul Travel

These stories and exercises help you find your true purpose, discover greater love than you've ever known, and learn that spiritual freedom is within reach.

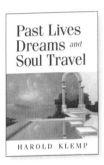

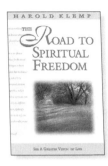

The Road to Spiritual Freedom, Mahanta Transcripts, Book 17

Sri Harold's wisdom and heart-opening stories of everyday people having extraordinary experiences tell of a secret truth at work in *your* life—there is divine purpose and meaning to every experience you have.

How to Survive Spiritually in Our Times, Mahanta Transcripts, Book 16

Discover how to reinvent yourself spiritually—to thrive in a changing world. Stories, tools, techniques, and spiritual insights to apply in your life now.

Autobiography of a Modern Prophet

This riveting story of Harold Klemp's climb up the Mountain of God will help you discover the keys to your own spiritual greatness.

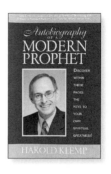

HU, the Most Beautiful Prayer

Singing *HU*, the ancient name for God, can open your heart and lead you to a new understanding of yourself. Includes a CD of the HU song.

Those Wonderful ECK Masters

Would you like to have *personal* experience with spiritual masters that people all over the world—since the beginning of time—have looked to for guidance, protection, and divine love? This book includes real-life stories and spiritual exercises to meet eleven ECK Masters.

The Sound of Soul

Sacred Sound, ancient mantra. HU is a universal love song to God; it brings alignment with your true purpose and highest good. This potent volume of contemplation seeds and spiritual exercises can get you started on the journey of a lifetime—your return to the heart of God.

Glossary

Words set in SMALL CAPS are defined elsewhere in this glossary.

Blue Light How the MAHANTA often appears in the inner worlds to the CHELA or seeker.

chela A spiritual student, often a member of ECKANKAR.

ECK The Life Force, Holy Spirit, or Audible Life Current which sustains all life.

Eckankar *EHK-ahn-kahr* The Path of Spiritual Freedom. Also known as the Ancient Science of SOUL TRAVEL. A truly spiritual way of life for the individual in modern times. The teachings provide a framework for anyone to explore their own spiritual experiences. Established by Paul Twitchell, the modern-day founder, in 1965. The word means Co-worker with God.

ECK Masters Spiritual Masters who can assist and protect people in their spiritual studies and travels. The ECK Masters are from a long line of God-Realized SOULS who know the responsibility that goes with spiritual freedom.

71

HU *HYOO*   The most ancient, secret name for God. It can be sung as a love song to God aloud or silently to oneself to align with God's love.

Living ECK Master   The spiritual leader of ECKANKAR. He leads SOUL back to God. He teaches in the physical world as the Outer Master, in the dream state as the Dream Master, and in the spiritual worlds as the Inner Master. SRI Harold Klemp became the MAHANTA, the Living ECK Master in 1981.

Mahanta   An expression of the Spirit of God that is always with you. Sometimes seen as a BLUE LIGHT or Blue Star or in the form of the Mahanta, the LIVING ECK MASTER. The highest state of God Consciousness on earth, only embodied in the Living ECK Master. He is the Living Word.

planes   Levels of existence, such as the Physical, Astral, Causal, Mental, Etheric, and SOUL Planes.

Soul   The True Self, an individual, eternal spark of God. The inner, most sacred part of each person. Soul can see, know, and perceive all things. It is the creative center of Its own world.

Soul Travel   The expansion of consciousness. The ability of SOUL to transcend the physical body and travel into the spiritual worlds of God. Soul Travel is taught only by the LIVING

ECK Master. It helps people unfold spiritually and can provide proof of the existence of God and life after death.

Sound and Light of ECK   The Holy Spirit. The two aspects through which God appears in the lower worlds. People can experience them by looking and listening within themselves and through Soul Travel.

Spiritual Exercises of ECK   Daily practices for direct, personal experience with the Sound Current. Creative techniques using contemplation and the singing of sacred words to bring the higher awareness of Soul into daily life.

Sri   A title of spiritual respect, similar to reverend or pastor, used for those who have attained the Kingdom of God. In Eckankar, it is reserved for the Mahanta, the Living ECK Master.

For more explanations of Eckankar terms, see *A Cosmic Sea of Words: The ECKANKAR Lexicon*, by Harold Klemp.

About the Author

Award-winning author, teacher, and spiritual guide Sri Harold Klemp helps seekers reach their full potential.

He is the Mahanta, the Living ECK Master and spiritual leader of Eckankar, the Path of Spiritual Freedom. He is the latest in a long line of spiritual Adepts who have served throughout history in every culture of the world.

Sri Harold teaches creative spiritual practices that enable anyone to achieve life mastery and gain inner peace and contentment. His messages are relevant to today's spiritual needs and resonate with every generation.

Sri Harold's body of work includes more than one hundred books, which have been translated into eighteen languages and won multiple awards. The miraculous, true-life stories he shares lift the veil between heaven and earth.

In his groundbreaking memoir, *Autobiography of a Modern Prophet*, he reveals secrets to spiritual success gleaned from his personal journey into the heart of God.

Find your own path to true happiness, wisdom, and love in Sri Harold Klemp's inspired writings.